WHAT YOU PRACTICE IS WHAT YOU HAVE

A GUIDE TO
HAVING THE LIFE YOU WANT

CHERI HUBER

AUTHOR OF **THERE IS NOTHING WRONG WITH YOU**

EDITED AND ILLUSTRATED BY JUNE SHIVER

ACKNOWLEDGMENTS

I want to express profound appreciation for the monks at the Zen Monastery Peace Center — Alex, Amy, Dave, Jen, Melinda, Michael, Sequoia — for their commitment to Zen awareness practice and to the Bodhisattva Vow. My own efforts are enhanced immeasurably by theirs.

For support in life-in-general, helping to free me up to write and meditate, big thank-yous to Bob Kayne, Brian Terrel, Jan Letendre, Marie Waters, and Rebecca McIlwain.

TABLE OF CONTENTS

INTRODUCTION

I started down this path many years ago with one ambition, to end suffering. I knew my understanding of what that meant was limited, but I was sure that whatever it meant, that was what I wanted to do. I loved the Bodhisattva Vow: to save all beings. That, I deeply felt, is something worth giving a life to. Later I came across this George Bernard Shaw quote:

"This is the true joy in life, the being used for a purpose recognized by yourself as a mighty one; to be thoroughly worn out before you are thrown on the scrap heap; the being a force of Nature instead of a feverish little clod of ailments and grievances complaining that the world will not devote itself to making you happy." (Man and Superman)

And there you have the young, idealistic, intensely passionate student of Zen who began this journey. I never wanted to teach, never wanted to write a book, never wanted students. I just wanted to meditate and save all beings.

As we all know, what we plan often has little to do with what happens. And so the teacher in the monastery where I trained as a monk sent me out to teach. After a few years of teaching, I wrote down the things I had been hearing myself say over and over, and they became our first book, *The Key and the Name of the Key Is Willingness.*

Through the years of teaching, each time I reached a new level of awareness in my practice, I was convinced that I had found the secret that would free people from their misery and open before them a path to freedom. Yes! This is it! Once they see through their depression, fear, confusion, and illusions they will be freed up to pursue a path of awakening! But it never worked that way. And I was always surprised.

About twenty years into my practice I came to this awareness: People will not wake up, let go, and be happy until they feel worthy. That's a central teaching of the Buddhist Precepts: We will not allow ourselves not to suffer if we are engaged in harmful behaviors. Once again, I was sure this was going to be the BINGO! heard round the world.

Soon, I began writing *Regardless of What You Were Taught to Believe, There Is Nothing Wrong With You: Going Beyond Self-Hate*. I was excited, convinced of the revolution that was about to engulf humanity (perhaps I exaggerate a bit). When people turned up in droves to find out more about ending self-hatred, I wanted to be there to assist them.

Did the revolution not make it to your neighborhood? Well, it didn't make it to most neighborhoods, although I cannot deny the profound impact that little book and the retreat by the same name have had on countless lives.

And so, once again, *What You Practice Is What You Have* points directly to this next level of practice, the themes I keep coming back to in the workshops and retreats I've taught for the last couple of years. As you perhaps read on the back cover, this book is a follow-up to *There Is Nothing Wrong With You*. I have attempted to write it so that it easily stands on its own, but I think the combination of both books will be powerful for those who are seeking release from suffering. What follows may seem repetitious for those who have been following along for a while. However, as Shunryu Suzuki Roshi famously pointed out, "If you lose the spirit of repetition, your practice will become quite difficult." Seeing again from a slightly different angle that which brings us joy can never be a hardship.

In gassho,
Cheri

WHAT THIS BOOK IS ABOUT

In *There Is Nothing Wrong With You: Going Beyond Self-Hate*, we explored the incessant voices in our heads telling us "There is something wrong with you" and "You should be more/better/different." Our shorthand for this is something wrong/not enough.

The key points in *There Is Nothing Wrong With You* are:

1) The hateful, judgmental voice in your head is not you. It is self-hate and it feeds on suffering.

2) It is possible not to believe what it says.

3) All the voice of self-hate wants is your energy, in any form it can lure you into giving it. If you struggle against the voice, it wins just as surely as if you believe it.

1

4) Willingness to practice mindful attentiveness and kindness for yourself can assist you to overcome self-hate.

In this book we take these next steps:

1) Learning to direct attention to the life experience we choose, a skill essential for "being in the driver's seat" in our own lives. It is literally how we become able to choose happiness. It is what we learn in meditation.

2) Finding and making real to ourselves a world without suffering.

If you encounter unfamiliar terms in your reading, please refer to the Glossary in the back. I include these definitions in almost all of these books. This time we added exercises so that you might have your own experience of what each of the following words is pointing at as we use them.

Awareness Practice
Subpersonalities
Beliefs and Assumptions
Projection
Disidentification
Centering
True Nature
Egocentric Karmic Conditioning
Self-Hate

LIGHT ROOM DARK ROOM

TWO "REALITIES"

There are two primary "realities" most people live in. I call these the

LIGHT ROOM

and the

DARK ROOM

I find it helpful to look at every event* as either happening in one of the rooms or as a potential portal into one of the two rooms.

*There is no such thing as a discrete event in life; every event is a piece of, cause of, and result of everything else in life, all occurring simultaneously.

LIGHT ROOM

We are born into what I call the Light Room. Children, before they are socially conditioned, and animals live in the Light Room, in the HERE and NOW. Not feeling separate from life, they are present to whatever is in the moment. Everything is new and interesting. They are spontaneous, rapidly moving from thing to thing as something fresh captures their attention.

Because they are not taking things personally, when children fall and skin a knee, they express their feelings about that and quickly return to the next fascinating adventure. They are one with life. Left to themselves they have no trouble with the Zen admonition to "eat when hungry, sleep when tired."

well-being

oneness

unconditional love

present moment
awareness

compassion

everything
is as is

peace
and
joy

wholeness

All
That
Is

kindness

nonseparate
reality

Acceptance of all
that arises.

As adults, when we are living in the Light Room, it is with a sense of well-being and belonging, of "rightness" that includes the range of human experience. Circumstances are no longer perceived as right or wrong; they simply are.

There are no mistakes. What happens just happens. We see what we see, learn what we learn, and feel grateful for our opportunities. We are sympathetic and understanding. Compassion is our orientation toward ourselves, others, and all of life. The statement, "All is One" makes perfect sense. In the Light Room, wisdom is recognized and comprehended; clarity replaces confusion; resistance is replaced by willingness, enthusiasm, and confidence. In the Light Room, nothing about life necessarily changes; it's our relationship to life that changes.

After the Zen master Bankei had passed away, a blind man who lived near Bankei's temple told a friend: "Since I am blind, I cannot watch a person's face, so I must judge character from the sound of the voice. Ordinarily when I hear someone congratulate another upon happiness or success, I also hear a secret tone of envy. When condolence is expressed for the misfortune of another, I hear pleasure and satisfaction, as if the one condoling was really glad there was something left to gain in his own world. In all my experience, however, Bankei's voice was always sincere. Whenever he expressed happiness, I heard nothing but happiness, and whenever he expressed sorrow, sorrow was all I heard." (Zen Flesh, Zen Bones)

Bankei lived in the LIGHT ROOM.

DARK ROOM

As we are socialized, we are pushed into the "Dark Room" of the illusion of a separate self, the world of egocentric karmic conditioning.

We are there before we know it. It is difficult
to get out, in that our extrication must be
volitional and we must swim against the tide.
For most, only suffering provides the will to get
out of the Dark Room.

Life in the Dark Room is one of
self-consciousness,
self-improvement,
self-judgment,
and self-hatred.

It is a life devoted
to serving and pleasing an imaginary entity,
an illusion, a fictional separate self
that is rooted in dissatisfaction
by nature of its false existence
and its attempt to have a life
outside All That Is.

It is a life of suffering.

Suffering is the experience of the Dark Room, suffering maintains the Dark Room, and suffering is the excuse for keeping a person in the Dark Room.

For example: Someone innocently says something to me that "hurts my feelings." Was I already in the Dark Room, perhaps lost in a story of something wrong/not enough when the comment arrived? Did the self-talk that started up support the belief that there's something wrong with me and take the comment as more proof?

If all of that transpires in unconsciousness, I will continue my stay in the Dark Room. If I was not in the Dark Room when the comment came in but was distracted so that unmonitored attention was drawn to an egocentric karmically conditioned reaction, I get a Free Pass into the Dark Room.

Being in the Dark Room is the same as being "identified." You are identified as an ego-self. You believe that egocentric karmic conditioning is who you are.

How can you tell if you're identified?

You are suffering.
You have a problem.
You are confused.
You are struggling.
You are complaining.
You are dissatisfied.
You believe there is something wrong.
You believe there is not enough.
You are fearful.

The only solution to

suffering,
  problems,
    confusion,
      struggles,
        complaining,
          dissatisfaction,
            something wrong,
              not enough,
              and fear

is to get out of the **DARK ROOM.**

The great difficulty is that the illusion of
a self that is separate from life WANTS
problems, confusion, struggles, dissatisfaction,
loss, lack, deprivation, wrongs, and fear. And
wants to complain about them loud and long.
That is where "its" life is.

It has its illusory existence when you bring it into an appearance of reality by focusing your attention and awareness on it.

It doesn't matter what it takes
to grab your attention;
getting and keeping your attention
is its life.

The more you suffer,
the more "life" it has.
When you give it your attention,
it feeds off your life force.

"Self reproach is painful; but the very pain is a reassuring proof that the self is still intact; so long as attention is fixed on the delinquent ego, it cannot be fixed on God and the ego (which lives upon attention and dies only when that sustenance is withheld) cannot be dissolved in the divine Light." (Aldous Huxley, *The Perennial Philosophy*)

All suffering is maintained
in a conversation with conditioning.

Do not be surprised if the conversation is about
something that makes you unhappy.

Your unhappiness is not *its* unhappiness.

We all know what it's like to be in the Light Room for moments, days, or longer, even though the voices of self-hate would argue that such a lofty height is unavailable to us.

AS ALWAYS T·H·E VOICES LIE!

We spend a great deal of life in the
LIGHT ROOM.
After all, it is our authentic nature.

But because our attention is habitually given over to maintaining egocentric karmic conditioning/self-hate, we are repeatedly convinced that the assessment of those voices is accurate, in spite of our experience. We call this "choosing our beliefs over our experience."

We must sympathize with ourselves for believing those voices. In many ways the Dark Room feels much more real and authentic than the Light Room. It seems—*though it is not the case*—that the Dark Room was our first experience of life and the Light Room is now being added. Exactly the opposite is the case. First, we were in the Light Room, and then, as we were socialized, we were talked into the Dark Room. We were talked out of the Light Room before our verbalizing and comprehending abilities developed.

To increase time spent in the Light Room, I encourage the following:

⇒ practicing with the five processes of subpersonalities, beliefs and assumptions, projection, disidentification, and centering (see glossary)

⇒ developing the ability to recognize and not believe self-hating voices

⇒ increasing our ability to direct attention to the life experience we want to be having

⇒ surrounding ourselves with reminders of inspiration, goodness, and possibility,

⇒ participating in workshops, retreats, and service projects with others who are practicing awareness in the Light Room.

EXERCISE

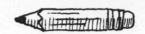

Draw a line down the middle of a piece of paper. Label one side Dark Room and the other Light Room. Fill each side with examples from your life.

THE "I" VOICE AND THE "YOU" VOICE

If you notice, the voice in your head has two "forms." Keep in mind that before a person has done a bit of awareness practice these distinctions are not apparent.

THE "I" VOICE

Generally speaking, subpersonalities refer to themselves as "I." When you hear, and believe, an "I" voice, suspect that you are identified with a particular aspect of yourself. When you hear an "I" voice, "you" are talking to "yourself" and call yourself "I." You discuss something with and for the benefit of yourself. For instance: "I know I should call her. It would be the right and fair thing to do, but I don't want to. I know, I'll get a coffee and maybe a little treat and I'll call her then. That won't be so bad."

In this little scene any of a number of subpersonalities could be talking. It could be the person with the job talking about a coworker or a youngster talking about mom. It could be a responsible, burdened person required to take care of unpleasant business. Who might it be for you?

THE "YOU" VOICE

Here, "you" might be listening to a voice in your head giving "you" information. That would go something like this: "It's cowardly of you not to call her. It's really rotten to leave her up in the air. How would you feel if someone did that to you? You're just being selfish."

With this voice, notice two interesting points:

1. Calling you "you" is a clue that it views itself as other than you—the person being talked to. This is very different from the "I know I should call her" conversation of the "I" voice. That conversation sounds like a person talking to her/himself. But the "you" voice (the subject) is talking to another person (the object).

2. There's distinct judgment in the "you" voice's use of "cowardly," "rotten," and "selfish." Its opinion of "you" is no mystery.

Judgment, criticism, comparison, and chastising are how the "you" voice—egocentric karmic conditioning/self-hate—communicates. When we practice turning attention to it, we begin to hear its "I am talking to you because I am not you and I don't approve of how you are and will now tell you what's wrong with how you are and how you should be different" tone. Here, the implied, perceived, and *believed* distance between the illusion of a separate self and the human shows up. The human, the incarnation, is addressed as a difficult child and spoken to as the problem in life: "If you would just be how you should be, my (imaginary!) life would be fine."

Vicious, huh?

It is difficult for conditioned humans to see egocentric karmic conditioning's talk about how it is victimized by "your" bad behavior as

For instance, the voice says, "You really are hopeless. You're never going to amount to anything. You just keep making bad decisions. You should call a monastery and see if they'll let you be a monk."

The message here is clear, yes?
You are so hopeless
you might as well go to a monastery.
This is aimed at making you feel very bad,
toss you right into the Dark Room.
It is not meant to help you!

But suppose you said, "Okay, that's a good idea. I'm going to call them." Would that voice say, "Oh, now you're getting somewhere. Finally you're seeing the light. Maybe there's some hope for you after all. Yes, call!"

Absolutely not.

Its only object
was to make you feel bad
and get a good long stay in the Dark Room,
not for you to feel good, inspired, and decisive.

Seconds after you decided to pick up the phone the voice would say, "Are you crazy? You can't go to a monastery! You have responsibilities! What would people think? What about your poor mother? You are so selfish!"

If you listen closely you will begin to hear that this is the same voice that beats you up for what it talked you into doing.

Are you with me? If you have doubts, practice noticing the "you" voice to prove to yourself who is who and what is what.

It is critical that you get it, from the beginning, now and forever, in all circumstances,

this life is yours!

The voices of self-hate, the ones that call you "you," try to steal it from you, and probably often succeed, but that doesn't change the fact that your life is yours to have and enjoy.

FINDING YOUR MENTOR

WORKING OUT YOUR OWN SALVATION

By turning attention to the voices that take over our lives, we can see the causes of suffering, and by bringing that suffering into the light of our inherent kindness and wisdom, we are freed from it. That is the process of using awareness practice to wake up and end suffering. We accomplish this in part through conscious mentoring.

The mentor is the centered awareness that allows us to observe and acknowledge conditioning without indulging in a self-hating reaction to it. We become our own mentor when we practice loving acceptance of whatever we discover in ourselves.

The Buddha taught that we each have one person to save: ourselves. We are told his final words were, "You must work out your own salvation diligently." That can sound like a daunting task until we understand what's involved in the process. What we are being guided to do is cease to identify with the ego-self, recognize our authentic nature, an expression of the intelligence that animates all...

and from that place of conscious, compassionate awareness embrace into unconditional love the incarnation that has believed itself to be that separate ego self.

The movement from being mentored to being the mentor is "how" a person can "work out your own salvation diligently."

In a flash of intuitive grace you find, at last, unconditional love and acceptance for the you that you were taught to see as a sinner, the "despicable" person that self-hate has beaten, and in that moment of acceptance and unconditional love you realize that "sinner" is actually a saint who has been teaching you how to love unconditionally.

And, in that moment of intuitive grace it is possible to realize that "you" are the saint, the sinner, the unconditional love and acceptance, and the awareness that contains and perceives all of it. That is a powerful moment of disidentification.

SAINT
AND
SINNER

Of course, it doesn't last. The clarity fades and once again life as usual takes hold. "I" am someone who had a powerful experience of "clarity." That process of remembering and forgetting is the reason for awareness practice. Someone asked, "If we are inherently enlightened, why do we need to practice?" The answer was, "Because you don't know you're inherently enlightened."

Awareness practice, waking up to our inherent enlightenment, is much like sailing across a large body of water. In sailing, we set our course, we sail along, we see where we are, we check where we are against where we're headed, and we adjust our course repeatedly. If we can see our destination we have a constant reference point; I'm tacking toward that mountain visible on the horizon. If we cannot

see our destination we must use less obvious signs—the path of the sun, the patterns of the stars at night—until we get a clear enough view to keep watch on our object. When the destination is not in sight, our tacking is much broader; when we can see where we're going, the adjustments become quite subtle.

Most of us begin awareness practice with a vague sense of destination and route. Often we face the equivalent of thinking we need to sail across the ocean while reading our instructions from a book! It's much kinder to the fledgling sailor first to practice sailing on a pond. When you get your sea legs under you, you will seek and enjoy greater challenges. No hurry.

It's the process that's the joy,
not the challenge or the destination.

Now, to bring this full-circle, it is time to get to know your sailing instructor: the mentor. The mentor is a recognizable representation of the wisdom, love, and compassion that is your authentic nature, center, that which animates, and cannot be reduced to the knowable. We all "know" what it means to be alive, we see life everywhere, we recognize instantly when life no longer animates a particular form. But of course we don't know. People make up all sorts of stories about life. Science breaks down all the components attempting to get to the essence. The religious and philosophical try to reach conclusions about the cause from the effect. But no one actually knows. We think we know, but we do not know. We might think we know what wisdom, love, and compassion is, but we don't. However, the fact that we don't know what it is does not mean it cannot and will not inform our lives. It can and it does.

Realizing that life animates form in a range of ways we can see and not see—life and death

35

happen within LIFE—does not constitute knowing what life is. Nor will I attempt to explain that here or anywhere! Our only point is that it is possible to drop the illusion of being a self separate from All That Is, and to allow life to live us. The intelligence that is "me" can, will, and does live this form called Cheri perfectly for as long as this particular form exists. "I," the imaginary small ego self that appears to exist separate from the rest of life, can have whatever issues and opinions about that it wants to cling to and will suffer accordingly, but it remains extraneous and irrelevant. Only life is. And only life can, and does, sail our little boats perfectly. We are not creating something new here; we are just waking up to what is.

EXERCISE

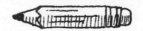

Consider the qualities and characteristics of the person you would want to have support and guide you. Write down those descriptions. Hint: Review a list of the people you most admire and respect, write down exactly what you value about them. See if these are the qualities you want to guide you in your life. (Remember, this is a projection exercise. The qualities you see in someone else are your qualities. When you see them "outside" it is a direct link to finding them "inside.")

Once you have a list of characteristics that comprise the ideal mentor for you, take a moment to get a mental picture of your mentor. Just close your eyes and allow the images to arise; don't *think* about it, just let the pictures flow past your mind's eye. The important thing here is not how your mentor looks, but how you feel in the presence of your mentor. Having a mental picture of this supportive, clear, non-judgmental, kind guide can strengthen your sense of relationship. When someone you love walks into a room you feel their presence through all the senses you have available to you. It can be helpful to practice recognizing your mentor's presence in the same way. How do you feel when the mentor is with you? What does the mentor "sound" like when communicating with you? If the mentor does not seem to have a physical form, make one up! Often people will say to me when I ask about the voices directing their emotions and behavior, "I don't hear anything. It's just a feeling." My response is, "That's fine, but what does that feeling mean? What is the feeling telling you?" It becomes quickly apparent that the person knows exactly what that feeling is communicating.

A CRUCIAL RELATIONSHIP

There is a crucial relationship between the
mentor and the skill of directing the attention.

The mentor

is access to the conscious, compassionate
awareness that animates. Moving from being
mentored to being the mentor is the movement
from an identity as a small ego-self to
awareness of oneself as compassionate being.

Directing the attention

allows one to withdraw attention from the
control of egocentric karmic conditioning, where
it's being used to maintain the illusion of
separation and suffering, and to return it to
conscious compassionate awareness.

Here are some statements of intention to assist in practicing withdrawing attention from egocentric karmic conditioning and returning to the compassionate awareness of the mentor. You may choose to add your own.

I will no longer allow my attention to be directed toward a perception of myself as someone trapped in a life that is beyond my control, helpless to affect my circumstances, working and trying hard but endlessly frustrated by failure, plagued by fear, anger, sadness, and depression, desperately seeking any escape offered, feeling bad and guilty about my inadequacy, beaten regularly by voices that see me as worthless and contemptible.

I will instead direct my attention to my own experience of the deepest desire of my heart, I will choose to attend to kindness, peace, acceptance, and compassion, embracing into unconditional love and acceptance all parts of me that suffer, and from that place of gratitude and generosity, practice embracing all life in the same way.

I will begin to practice recognizing when I am in the Dark Room of egocentric karmic conditioning/self hate and when I am in the Light Room of This/Here/Now. I will practice turning my attention away from the limited, negative, something wrong/not enough of the Dark Room and to the expansiveness and possibility of the Light Room. Although I will regularly get distracted, fooled, and bamboozled and will allow my attention to be hi-jacked by egocentric karmic conditioning/self-hate, as soon as I realize that has happened I will immediately turn my attention to what I want for my life, to lovingkindness and compassion, to peace and well-being.

I will give no attention to the voices of recrimination, judgment, criticism, or punishment.

I will surround myself with support for a life in the Light Room, seeking inspiration and strength from Sangha,* participate in what is up-lifting, prioritize what takes care of the heart, and surround myself with that which mirrors the unconditional love and goodness I know to be my true nature.

*Each individual's own source of kindred spirits, consciously journeying on a path of self-realization

DIRECTING THE ATTENTION

LEARNING TO DIRECT THE ATTENTION

This is what the Buddha had to say about "Right Attention":

"Right attention follows from right effort. It means keeping the mind where it should be. The wise train the mind to give complete attention to one thing at a time, here and now. Those who follow me must be always mindful, their thoughts focused on the dharma day and night. Whatever is positive, what benefits others, what conduces to kindness or peace of mind, those states of mind lead to progress; give them full attention. Whatever is negative, whatever is self-centered, what feeds malicious thoughts or stirs up the mind, those states of mind draw one downward; turn your attention away."

We could interpret the Buddha's words as guidance to...

GET OUT OF THE CONVERSATION IN YOUR HEAD!

BLAH BLAH BLAH

JABBER JABBER JABBER

When we first learn to sit in meditation, the undisciplined attention flits about from thing to thing. Classic descriptions liken the movement of attention to clouds floating by or a monkey swinging through the jungle from tree to tree. Through meditation and awareness practice we learn to direct the attention.

As our sitting practice deepens, we find ourselves increasingly able to bring attention back to the breath, to here, to now, to this. We become aware that attention rests with awareness more often and for longer periods. Soon, rather than coming back to the breath, we are able to stay with the breath.

Before long we notice that even when we are not sitting in meditation the attention is present with awareness. We feel the body walking and the breath moving in the body; we see colors and textures, hear sounds, feel the sun or the air on the skin, no longer "coming to" after an extended time "lost in thought," unaware of where we are or where we've been. We are here/now, and we are aware of being so.

Until directing the attention is mastered, awareness practice is primarily an intellectual activity. Sadly, the vast majority of aspirants never move beyond the stage of looking to conditioned mind to "understand" practice. Without good guidance and strong support, awareness practice is left to egocentric karmic conditioning/self-hate and the process is ill-fated and often cruel.

When egocentric karmic conditioning assumes the role of spiritual guide, we call it Pseudo Zen Master.

SOTO ZEN

CHOP WOOD

CARRY WATER

PSEUDO ZEN

"Chop wood, carry water" is so simple. You complicate things. You're not a good Zen student.

We are doomed to be victims of egocentric karmic conditioning until we take charge of our attention. The attention of a thoroughly conditioned adult human, which most of us are before awareness practice, is firmly in the grip of egocentric karmic conditioning. But we don't know that. It doesn't feel like that. What it feels like is "me just going around in life." We don't experience our attention *being turned* to thing after thing after thing; it seems as if we are doing the turning. The tricky part is that egocentric karmic conditioning is turning the attention and we think *it* is who we are.

Only when we step back into awareness and observe attention can we experience the difference between consciously directed attention and unconsciously manipulated attention.

Developing the skill of directing the attention can be practiced anywhere, any time. Remembering to practice directing the attention is itself a practice of directing the attention. Saying to yourself, silently or aloud, "I am directing my attention to..." is a powerful wake-up, get-here-now tool.

Let's take this for a test drive. Please do the following attention and awareness exercise and answer the questions.

EXERCISE

Look around. Move your attention until you find something white in your environment. Be aware of looking at the white for one full breath and then resume reading.

Did your attention stay on the white for the full breath? Were you *aware* of *attending* to the white?

This time close your eyes, then open them and be aware of moving your attention until you find something red in your environment. Look at it for two long, full breaths, and then close your eyes for a breath before returning to the reading.

What did you notice? Did you sense the relationship between attention and awareness? Can you sense that attention is how you observe awareness and awareness is how you observe attention?

Now turn your attention to your ears. With your attention on your ears, see if you can feel the breath moving in your body. Next, turn your attention to your ears, feel the breath moving in your body, and sense how attention is moving around in the field of awareness.

After considering this exercise for a few minutes, bring the attention back to the breath, to the present, where life is happening.

WHY LEARN TO DIRECT ATTENTION?

There is everything to recommend learning to direct the attention and nothing against it!

1. It's practical. When you need to stay attentive to something or someone—at work, in a challenging conversation—you can do it.

2. It's entertaining. You can make up all sorts of little games for yourself such as turning your attention to particular colors or objects and using them as reminders to turn your attention to the breath, to yourself with a kind word, etc.

3. It's relaxing. With your attention going where you choose rather than habitually to the stressful conversations of conditioned mind, stress and tension no longer have access to you.

4. It's efficient. When it's time to meditate formally, you are way ahead of the game by having practiced being present all day long!

5. It's fun. Life is fun. Conditioned mind and the voices of self-hate are not fun. When you give your attention to life, your fun quotient goes way up.

6. It's kind. When you are not lost in an unconscious relationship with the negativity of egocentric karmic conditioning, you become a pleasure to be around. You are a gift to the world.

7. It's simple. Anyone with sufficient capacity and willingness can do it. "Now, I will turn my attention to..." No complex rules, no standards&easy.

8. It brings immediate gratification. Each moment you are HERE/NOW is a moment of well-being. Practice directing your attention ten times today and you have ten experiences of well-being. Tomorrow twenty, then thirty, then much of your day, then most of your day...

9. It's a guilt-free pleasure. You can be enjoying this little awareness game all the time and no one will ever know what you're doing. They will just enjoy you more because you're more pleasant to be around.

10. It's safer. For example, you're less likely to have an accidental fall or be surprised by oncoming traffic when you're present where you are.

11. It's a guarantee. The voices can't as easily "get you" for having made mistakes (not that it's possible to make mistakes). When attention is focused on the task at hand, you're less likely to do things that the voices will talk you into feeling bad about.

BANK STATEMENT

OVERDRAWN

12. It's restful. You're able to get to sleep easier when attention is on the breath and not off in a story that gets you all wound up.

Breath in
Breath out
z z z z

I shouldn't blah blah too bad jabber jabber

13. It's easier to be around others. Putting attention on the love you have for someone, including yourself, makes it easier to accept them as they are. It's a relief when you don't waste attention on judgment and disappointment.

14. It's like being at home. Like Dorothy in *The Wizard of Oz*, no matter how daunting the circumstances, the practice of directing attention, along with the willingness to see whatever arises inside, leads to the fullest, most joyful life imaginable.

15. It's a calming constant, a certainty.

There are probably many more good reasons for practicing directing the attention. Can you think of some?

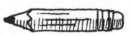

WHAT YOU DO IS WHAT YOU GET

What we focus on
is what we have.

If while learning to play the piano my unconscious mantra is "I will never be good at this," what I'll get out of playing the piano is the belief that I will never be good at it.

Does that mean I won't be good at it? I'll probably never know, because regardless of what anyone else says about my playing, my experience will be "not good at this."

Why is this?

Because one process
does not lead to another.

Believing I'll never be a good pianist,
regardless of how much I practice,
results only in continuing to
believe I'll never be a good pianist.

Worrying about the future
won't help me have a better future.
Worrying about the future will help me have
a future of worrying about the future!

The only thing
I will ever get from life
is what I am doing
—what I am *practicing*—
in the moment.
What I do is what I get.

The *Random House Unabridged Dictionary* defines practice with phrases such as "habitual or customary performance; repeated performance or systematic exercise for the purpose of acquiring skill or proficiency; the action or process of performing or doing something; to perform or do habitually or usually; to train or drill."

The dictionary definitions of practice assume a level of conscious intention. I consciously intend to practice drawing to get better at it. I consciously intend to practice speaking Spanish to increase my proficiency. I repeat something regularly for the purpose of enhancing my skill. I'm aware of what I'm doing and why I'm doing it.

For most of us, what we practice unconsciously has a much larger place in our lives than what we practice with conscious intention. From the time we get up in the morning to when we go to bed at night, we practice something. A morning routine, choosing what to wear, backing out of the driveway, going to work, relaxing in the evening—very little of what conditioned humans do in a day is random or spontaneous. What we eat, where we eat, when we eat, how we eat, with whom we eat—all much more scripted and programmed than we like to think. Even if you seldom eat at the same places or with the same people, notice how little flexibility there is in how you approach mealtime.

These are activities that you probably never think of as something you are practicing. A clue to identifying them is that they raise all kinds of resistance when interfered with: your morning routine; how you approach errands or chores; the way you keep your possessions; rewards or treats; how you are with money.

So we can think of habits and routines as practices. We also practice other things, such as believing things that aren't true, denying the evidence right before our eyes, judging ourselves and others, believing the conversations in the head (worry; fantasy; reviewing disappointments or "failures," imagining future events; viewing horrific scenes of injury or death of loved ones; visions of financial ruin; an old-age of sickness and destitution; embarrassing situations; injustices; wrongs...).

Without awareness of our unconscious practices, we have little chance of freeing ourselves from the suffering they cause. So, practicing being aware of where attention habitually goes and the suffering it causes and practicing finding the willingness to direct attention to the experience of life we want to be having are powerfully helpful as we work out our own salvation diligently.

If your attention is on anything other than the life experience you want to be having, that's what you're *practicing* and that's what you have.

If you don't understand that there is no "I," no single, unchanging individual, you're *practicing* ignorance and delusion.

If you assume false beliefs about you are true, you're *practicing* believing something is wrong with you.

If you don't understand projection, you're *practicing* believing the world you create moment-by-moment is objective reality and that it is everybody else's world too.

If you don't know that it's possible to disidentify, you are *practicing* believing that the suffering reality you're in is all that is possible.

If you don't know that who you authentically are does not suffer and has no need for beliefs, you are *practicing* believing that the separate self is real and that suffering is inevitable.

EXERCISE

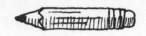

1. Make a list of things you practice, or have practiced, with conscious intention in order to increase your skill or enjoyment.

2. Make a list of some of the automatic, habitual practices you engage in regularly without being consciously aware that you are doing them.

3. Make a list of awareness practices you have freely chosen and that you engage in regularly.

Remember: We are practicing awareness. We are not problem-solving, blame-laying, or creating self-improvement plans. We are just watching to see what is so.

WHAT ARE YOU PRACTICING NOW?

The voices of conditioning would have us believe that we can't take on something as big as practicing awareness. "I can't pay attention all the time! I'm too busy. Besides, paying attention is exhausting."

It is true that paying attention all the time is exhausting—for egocentric karmic conditioning. When you are unconscious, lost in conditioned thought loops, caught up in a conversation with the voices in your head (a one-sided conversation, since you're primarily the listener), conditioned mind is at the center of the universe, completely content.

As you attend, you will notice the voices in your head and the voices of society follow a very similar pattern, a pattern designed to maximize the amount of attention going to maintaining the illusory world of egocentric karmic conditioning and a minimum amount of attention going to maintaining you and the life you could have without it.

It does not take more effort to pay attention to you, to the breath, to here/now. It's not a matter of more or less; it's a matter of choice.

You can give your attention to the endless, repetitive yammering of the voices in your head telling you what's wrong, what's missing, how you should be but are not, how your life is not working and never will,

or you can give your attention to where you are, to who you are, and to practicing having a life of joy, abundance, and inspiration.

PAYING ATTENTION:
MONASTERY DISCUSSION

Monk: Lately I've been hearing, and often believing, the voice that says how unlikable I am compared to other people. This comes up every time I'm here in group discussion.

Cheri: Here's a cut-to-the-chase question: What will it take to get you to turn your attention away from that voice? Because there's no other solution. There's nothing to understand, it's not going to change, it's not going away, you're not going to improve enough that it stops. There's no alternative to turning your attention away from it! It's actually comforting to discover the only thing that will work! So, what's it going to take? Can I pay you? (laughter)

Monk: I think I'm really getting it that the voices...um...that it's, um...

Cheri: Is "crap" the word you're looking for?

Monk: There's no pleasing it. If I say A, it's wrong. If I say B, it's wrong. If I say anything, I'm slammed.

Cheri: Oh, yes, all roads lead to "slammed."

Monk: Yeah, that's good to know.

Cheri: Truly! I wish I knew a clearer and more effective way to say it. A way to say it that would lead someone to say "oh, I see" and be transformed. But the reality is it is completely mechanical. A hateful voice says something designed to make me feel bad, I step back and bring my attention to center, to the present moment of sensory awareness, the experience of here and now. The voice says something else, I look back to center. Over and over. Pretty soon I get ahead of the game. I just stay in center, with my attention on what is right in front of me. Self-hate is still in the background, doing whatever it's doing, but I'm no longer giving it attention. There's no sense in trying to stop the conversation or appease the voice. It needs to be completely ignored. So when that thought-train leaves the station, you simply don't get on. Just let it go on by. That's what needs to happen.

Monk: OK, I'll practice that.

Cheri: Take it on as a goal. Say to yourself something like five minutes out of every hour I'm going to stop and turn my attention away from the conversation in my mind, regardless of what it is, and turn my attention to where I want it to be. Then practice for 10 minutes. Practice turning the attention until it's just how you live, as automatic as brushing your teeth. Those voices are always going to say the same things. Always. And so we practice turning the attention exactly as we would practice playing tennis or the piano. Repetition. Dedication. Love.

ENTERING THE PORTAL

Once you are fairly proficient in remembering that you choose to direct the attention* and in directing the attention once you remember, you can make use of the portal into the Light Room that we refer to as "the gap." The gap is the tiny space found in transitions, at the top of the inhalation before the exhalation begins, at the bottom of the exhalation, before the next breath begins, when one thought fades and before another appears, as the attention moves from thing to thing...

That tiny space where "nothing is happening" is a doorway into the Light Room.

*Keep in mind that sitting meditation practice is the best support you can have in gaining that proficiency.

"THE GAP" GUIDED IMAGERY - RECORDED AT THE MONASTERY

Cheri: We're going to practice turning attention to "the space between." Please close your eyes and I'll take you through a short guided meditation.

Everyone please exhale... and at the top of your next inhalation look for that little gap... and then exhale when you're ready... get to the bottom, and there's the little gap... notice if any conversation wants to start about how well you're doing with this exercise so far... It could be that you're aware as you attend to the gaps that there are no thoughts...

OK. Open your eyes, please. What happened? Could you feel it? Did you find the gap?

1st person: I was watching and a voice said you did it wrong. You were breathing too quickly and had to backtrack to stay with the instructions.

Cheri: So you believed the voice that said you did it wrong.

1st person: Yes, I guess I did because I immediately started trying to do what the voice was telling me to do. I went where I thought the breath was supposed to be.

Cheri: And missed the gap altogether, right? The gap was conveniently filled with conversation about how you were doing the exercise wrong, which is a really fast trip out of the gap. Very good. Thank you.

2nd person: When I got to the gap it felt like a velvety darkness with stars. Then the voice said that can't be it, the gap doesn't look like that.

Cheri: Heavens no! The gap doesn't look like that! What were you thinking?

3rd person: When I went to the gaps I would think, is this center? It doesn't feel ecstatic!

Cheri: Oh, I didn't get the memo that center feels ecstatic! I'll be darned. So you get to the gap and then the voice says no that can't be it, it doesn't feel like it should. That's perfect, isn't it? We get to the gap and then we get what keeps us from being in the gap.

4th person: The habit is to look to my thoughts to see if I'm having any thoughts.

Cheri: Yes, that's the "I" who is in charge of "getting it," of understanding, and that's never going to happen. It's never going to get it. That's why ego puts it in charge of getting it.

The instant it occurs to you
that you're in the Dark Room,
you've already made the shift
to the Light Room.

When you turn attention
to the gap,
to HERE/NOW,
to That Which Animates,
to peace, presence, compassion,
kindness, beauty, goodness...
you are in the Light Room.

HOW DO YOU WANT YOUR LIFE TO BE?

I project we have a reason for everything we do in life. There's a goal, an aim, a purpose. "Worldly goals" are freely stated and socially acceptable: "I want to make a lot of money." "I want to retire early." "I want a better life for my family." "I want to win the lottery." For most of you reading this book, I'm betting your motivations are more along the lines of: "I want to be a better person." "I want to be the best person I can." "I have a lot of flaws that need to be repaired." "I want to wake up and end suffering." "I want to make a difference in the world."

Whatever their goals, people work hard to meet them, only *assuming* they know what they're working hard for. And that *assumption* is the cause of incalculable suffering.

For example:

I work hard to make money to buy a house for my family, *assuming* that then I'll be happy. But the truth is all I get from working hard to make money is working hard to make money. What I really want is to be happy, not to work hard to make money to buy a big house.

More examples of assumptions:
If I were a better person, I'd be happy.
When I lose weight, I'll be happy.
If I had a _____, I'd be happy.
When _____, I'll be happy.
If only _____, I wouldn't worry so much.
If he would _____, I wouldn't get so angry.
If they were _____, I wouldn't have to work so hard.

HERE IS WHERE THE SUFFERING HAPPENS:

The biggest misunderstanding is the belief that one process leads to another. But one process does not lead to another.

Working hard does not lead to being happy.
"Working hard" is one process.
"Being happy" is another.

Losing weight does not lead to being happy.
Getting what you want does not lead to having the life you want.
Changing your environment does not lead to having the feeling you want.

All we ever get is what we do, what we practice.

HOW DO YOU WANT YOUR LIFE TO BE?
GUIDED IMAGERY

Let's consider for a few moments just what your motivation is for working and trying so hard. As you read, pause after each phrase as you follow the instructions. (Listen to this guided imagery, recorded by Cheri, online at www.livingcompassion.org/guided-imageries.)

Imagine that you have arrived at your destination. Your goal has been achieved. You have completed every course and your self really is improved! You have enough money, your family is comfortable, you don't have to go every day to a job you dislike, and you can devote yourself to activities you enjoy... Take a moment to picture yourself in your version of that "having arrived" scenario... Don't just see yourself there, *sense* yourself there... Take that scene from a snapshot to a movie, with you as the lead... You are having the life you always dreamed of... Take in everything you can about the situation... Notice how you're dressed and the expression on your face... Notice how your body moves... There you are, the star of the show, the one who has arrived, having the life you've always wanted...

How do you feel? What are the sensations in your body? What label fits those feelings? Are you at peace... satisfied... happy... comfortable...? Where do you feel that feeling in your body? If that feeling had a color, what color would it be? Close your eyes for a few moments and turn your attention to that feeling... Breathe the feeling into your whole body... See if you can find the exact center of the feeling and then expand it again... Let the color become more vibrant with each breath....

Stay with that experience for as long as you choose... After a few moments, open your eyes and continue reading.

Here is the mind-boggling, life-changing, freedom-providing point made via that little exercise:

⇨ Without completing another self-improvement course,

⇨ without doing all the things egocentric karmic conditioning says you *must* do to be an acceptable person,

⇨ without any beatings for failure to meet conditioning's standards,

⇨ precisely the way you are RIGHT NOW,

you experienced the life you want to have, the life you've been told you cannot have until after you jump through all the hoops!

But, if egocentric karmic conditioning
talked you out of doing the exercise,
all you have is
that same old PROMISE of a reward
for doing the hard work
it says you must do
before you can have the life you want
and feel what having that life
will allow you to feel!
A promise it will never keep.

A GENTLE NUDGE:

If egocentric karmic conditioning
talked you out of doing the exercise,
go back and do it before proceeding.

So, here's the question:

If you can have NOW the life experience you're being promised you will get to have somewhere out there in the future (after you have worked hard and been judged, beaten and abused for being the wrong person), if you can have that experience any time you turn your attention to it, if you can feel now the way you're being told you will feel then,

isn't it just kind of sensible to go on ahead and have that feeling right now?

*Can you imagine
any intelligent argument
for not having it right now?*

(If you heard an argument, you can be sure that's the voice of egocentric karmic conditioning/self-hate fighting for its survival.)

This is perhaps the best example of "one process does not lead to another."

A beating by self-hate
for not being the right person in this moment
is never going to lead
to having the life you want
somewhere out there in an imaginary future.

A beating will lead to more beatings.
Having the life you want
leads to having the life you want.
If you want to be happy,
turn your attention to your experience of happy,
and be happy.

BEING HAPPY
IS NOT DEPENDENT UPON
CONTENT OR CIRCUMSTANCES.

If the voices are trying to convince you it is irresponsible to be happy when you haven't earned it, when your character is not sufficiently improved, or if you're hearing there's a danger you will become self-indulgent (a projection from egocentric karmic conditioning/self-hate, it being both in spades), or that this is too simple or you're being fooled by some New Age nonsense...

well, consider the source.

The glaring fact is that
egocentric karmic conditioning
has its imaginary life,
and self-hate maintains
that imaginary life,
in getting you to believe that
their shenanigans are essential.

There will be no eagerness from that quarter
for you to prove to yourself that your freedom
is in your hands...

FREEDOM

and that
    being free
        is as simple as
            learning to
                direct your attention
                    moment by moment
                        to the life experience
                            you want to be having.

MEDITATION

HOW AND WHY

GET OUT OF THE CONVERSATION

Suffering is created and maintained in a conversation in the head. (It's also maintained in most of the conversation with those outside the head, particularly the media, which becomes obvious once the conversation inside the head is seen through and mastered.)

It's not possible to suffer without conversation, and conversation takes two people. The two are often 1) egocentric karmic conditioning/self hate, masquerading as "you" (usually doing the talking), and 2) a subpersonality that is usually being talked to. However, the conversation can also be between egocentric karmic conditioning and egocentric karmic conditioning, especially when there's a duality involved. For instance, "I don't want to go" (perhaps to meditation!), and "You should go."

The authentic human, your true nature, isn't a part of the conversation, though it is usually listening. It *seems* as if it's "me" "talking to myself," and egocentric karmic conditioning/self-hate is very, very happy to support that misconception. What you must do is to watch carefully enough to see that "you" —what you experience as your deepest sense of yourself— is the awareness that can observe the whole thing.

HOW TO GET OUT OF THE CONVERSATION

When I wanted to learn to meditate I found only two books on the subject. Now, there are vast amounts written on it. And even though I have contributed to those vast amounts, my encouragement is this: Don't attempt a formal sitting practice until you 1) are mostly free of self-hatred, and 2) can't stop yourself any longer and simply must sit in meditation.*

As I'm fond of pointing out, spiritual practice does not begin until the beatings stop. A voice berating you about how you meditate is not a part of meditation practice any more than a voice berating you about cooking or basketball has anything to do with those activities. The activity is the activity. The beating is the beating. Conditioned mind puts the two together and convinces a human that they *go* together.

---

* Also, awareness practice should not be attempted without a sense of humor.

Over the years I've taught many, many people to meditate who immediately put their practice in the hands of self-hatred, fell into increased misery and suffering, and soon quit all attempts. Even many who continue, in spite of all encouragement to the contrary, allow conditioned mind, in the form of Pseudo Zen to direct their practice.*

SOTO ZEN

When hungry, eat.

When tired, sleep.

PSEUDO ZEN

Zen says you should eat when you're hungry and sleep when you're tired.

*Technically, these references to meditation and practice should be in quotes since, as this book is meant to point out, being guided by conditioned mind is *practicing* being guided by conditioned mind. It has nothing to do with what sitting meditation practice is or does.

Here are simple guidelines for meditating.

Wear loose, comfortable clothing.

Use a meditation cushion or find a comfortable place to sit where your back can be straight.

If you use a chair, you will want your feet to be flat on the floor.

Neither slump back nor sit rigidly upright.

Align your shoulders to be directly over your hips and your head to be in line with your spine.

Place your hands in the cosmic mudra or rest them in your lap.

Let your abdomen relax.

Let your eyes go soft and unfocused, resting at a 45 degree angle about three feet in front of you.

Here is a short guided meditation. Either record it for yourself or listen online at http://www.livingcompassion.org/guided-imageries

Turn the attention to the breath... feel the breath move in the body... notice the air as it enters the body... feel the body expand to accommodate the breath... feel the body contract as the air is exhaled... just noticing... the abdomen rising and falling... the body resting against what is supporting it...

When you feel ready, as you exhale silently count one... with the next exhalation, count two... continue to ten and begin again at one...

When the attention wanders, as surely it will, just notice where it went and gently bring it back to the breath... continue noticing... notice thoughts as they arise... turn the attention back to the breath... notice sensations in the body... bring the attention back to the breath... notice emotions that arise... turn the attention back to the breath... notice the conversation conditioned mind attempts to introduce... bring the attention back to the breath... just breathing and noticing everything that arises... if judgments, criticisms, or comparisons are addressed to you, just notice them and come back to the breath... something arises, attention attends, you are aware of attention attending, you drop it all and return attention to the breath...

We are practicing
being aware of where attention is
and what it is attending to.

We are practicing
directing the attention
to what we want to attend to.

We are practicing
experiencing ourselves
as the awareness that is aware of it all.

I need a haircut. I'll call
and make an appointment.
I look like a shaggy dog.

OK. We'll call later. 1....
2.... 3.... 4.... 5.... 6....
7.... 8.... 9.... 10.... 1....
2.... 3....

You shouldn't have told
her you'd help with the
banquet. You'll never
learn, will you?

Hmm. Self-hate. 1....
2.... 3.... 4.... 5.... 6....
7.... 8.... 9.... 10.... 1....
2.... 3.... 4.... 5....

What a waste of time.
You're not going to get
your work done and
you won't get to...

Ah. Urgency. 1.... 2....
3.... 4....

I'm such a good and
disciplined meditator.

Yes, dear. 1.... 2.. 3....
4.... 5.... 6....

MEDITATION:
OPEN AIR DISCUSSION

Meditator: I notice when I'm meditating and daydreaming starts, the daydreams revolve around problems at work and things like that. They are in the background distracting me. It helps to say to myself to slow down and focus on the breath, to pay attention in minute detail.

Cheri: What you're doing with your meditation practice is committing to paying attention, to being present. Which is not to say that you need to have any particular experience. You're practicing bringing the attention back to the present, and you don't want to turn that into a series of "better ideas" about "things to help me be present." If you did, conditioned mind would really like to get hold of that. It would love to distract you with try this/try that, you could do this/you could do that. That's clearly not a helpful direction. So you're paying attention, you notice when you slide off, you say "okay," and you come right back to your commitment to focus on the breath.

Meditator: Makes a lot of sense. My experience has been pretty much that. I'm aware of what's going on, and then conditioned mind takes hold of it and tries to make an experience out of it, tries to make it mean that I'm "getting somewhere," which is a scam.

Cheri: Yes. The other part of what you're doing is developing a relationship with the guy who is doing the sitting. You're building a sense of gratitude, commitment, appreciation and compassion for the person sitting on the cushion attempting to do this practice. You're learning to be a wise, caring, supportive mentor. You're learning not to take that guy on the cushion personally. You are no longer identified as that small separate self. You are now the conscious compassionate awareness that can embrace him.

Meditator: Yes, I see. That's a missing part for

me, the relationship with this guy who is sitting there doing this. I don't know that I actually give him that compassion and appreciation for sitting there doing this, working through this.

Cheri: And that's increasingly what you will be learning and practicing. You will have a growing sense of what it is that leads you to sit, of what inspires you. It's as if you're being drawn home. Do you know what is guiding you there?

Meditator: There's definitely something. Every day that I go to sit I actually feel kind of excited.

Cheri: Exactly, and the more you sit, the stronger you will sense that who you are is that excitement. And the excitement is just one expression of that which animates you. We could call it intelligence; we could call it awareness, sensitivity, intuition, expansiveness. Whatever label we might want to put on it, you will begin to sense "Oh, that's it. That's the lovingkindness, that's the compassion." Then you look at that guy and the efforts he's making. You appreciate that he would go through what is required—pain, anxiety, going up against conditioning with its constant "I don't want to do this, I hate it"—and you sit in awe of his willingness and sincerity, all that he is. It's the same sense of admiration and appreciation that you would have for the person sitting on the cushion next to you in a retreat, or when you read the life of the great Zen masters of old. You think, "Wow, that is so amazing that anybody would do that."

Meditator: Yes, the praise I would give to someone else I forget to give to that guy in me who is doing this work, who is meditating.

Cheri: And there's nothing personal in it. As soon as you make that shift from identifying as him and into simply appreciating his sincerity, you can look at him and see who he truly is and love him unconditionally.

Meditator: Yes, I think the key in what you're saying is having compassion for the guy doing the sitting.

Cheri: Yes, you are here to embrace him in conscious, compassionate acceptance.

MEDITATION:
MONASTERY DISCUSSION

Retreatant: I haven't meditated before coming here for this retreat. If I go back home and decide to start a meditation practice...

Cheri: Don't *decide* to take up a meditation practice. We have to *know* what we want to do. Because, and here's something to prove to yourself, we always do what we want to do. It might not always seem like that. In a given situation we might not like our choices, but we'll always choose the one we prefer, unpalatable though it may be. So my encouragement is don't decide to meditate, to do awareness practice. Don't let it get on the "should" list. As soon as something gets on the should list, it's on the way out the door. If you don't want to meditate, don't meditate. If you understand that meditation is a huge piece of the ending suffering puzzle, and you want to end suffering, then you'll figure out how and when to do it, because it's what you want to do. As soon as you make that shift, it's easy.

Retreatant: I'm noticing that it's hard to stay with the breath just sitting here...

Cheri: Yes! It's the hardest thing in the world.

Retreatant: Does it get easier?

Cheri: Yes. The only reason it feels hard is because of the voices in your head. They're used to being in control of your life. They have your attention all the time. A voice is the last thing you hear before going to sleep and the first when you wake up. If you wake up in the night, it's there talking to you, right? About something unpleasant, right? It's always there. It's your constant, most intimate relationship, and it doesn't like to share you with anything. So you're starting down this track of... unfaithfulness. You're in danger of choosing yourself over it. And it doesn't want that to happen. We could say that it's a jealous lover, if it loved you, but it doesn't. It's a very jealous master, and it has no interest in your freedom. That's why we have to want to practice. We cannot do it because we should. Nobody will do it because they should.

With egocentric karmic conditioning we don't get to have our own life; we get to have what it tells us we can have... which is, for most people, abuse. But as soon as you say no, we're not doing that anymore, this is my life and I'm going to have it, I'm not going to live it for a parasite that wants to make it miserable for me. When we make that turn, when we can see that it is not who we are, we get our life back.

REMEMBERING...

For many the most difficult aspect of practice is remembering to do it. That can sound silly but it's true. Very sincere people go to bed each night vowing to have a different relationship with egocentric karmic conditioning the next day.

"I will meditate first thing."
"I will pay attention all day."
"I will stop often and come back to the breath."
"I will not believe the voices."

The next day passes without a single "dharmic" thought. Just as they are dozing off that night, the voice reminds them they were going to meditate, pay attention, and be present. "But you failed again," sneers the voice of self-hate. The hapless human drifts off to sleep feeling bad, believing itself to be a spiritual failure, an irredeemably lost soul, not realizing that they have just been hoodwinked by egocentric karmic conditioning one more time. "I'll do better tomorrow," the sincere, hard-working person sighs, somewhat doubtfully. Conditioning rubs its imaginary hands together in anticipation of more suffering ahead.

But here's what we can practice: Rubbing our very real hands together in anticipation of another day in which "failure" plays no part, whether we meet conditioning's standards or not.

Another day in which we choose
kindness over abuse.

Practice recognizing when you're not living in loving kindness and unconditional acceptance.

Practice recognizing when your attention has been hijacked by suffering, and drop it.

Practice directing attention to the experience you want.

Practice having the life you choose.

Remember:
You don't need to figure anything out.
You don't need to see how it all fits together.
All you need is to practice
directing your attention
to the life you want.

AN AMAZINGLY HELPFUL TOOL:

THE RECORDING

In *There Is Nothing Wrong With You*, the primary practice tool is a recording of "reassurances."

Reassurances are true statements made by one's mentor, or center. The statements are meant to solidify the relationship between the human being (you) and the wise, compassionate awareness (the "centered you") that is available to encourage and support us through life when we turn our attention to it.

In this book, the primary practice tool for learning to direct attention is another recording in which the mentoring process expands. This recording may include your reassurances, but that is not the primary purpose. Here is how to take the next step:

In your own voice,
make a recording that reminds you
of everything you need to remember
so that you can make
the choices you know
you need to make,
from center,
to have the life you know
is possible for you.

Put anything in your recording that speaks to your heart. Much of what you might choose to record may come from outside sources, but nothing counts until we take it in and get it for ourselves.

Of course, the recording can consist of anything you choose, but I will offer a few suggestions that I've found helpful.

YOUR RECORDING: THE CONTENT

--Reminders for body, mind, and emotions:
Use this section to keep in the front of your conscious awareness all those commitments, choices, and decisions that conditioning distracts you from. Write down your responses to these questions, if you'd like.

How do you want to treat your body?

How do you want to approach food and drink?

What are your commitments to exercise and fitness?

How will you support yourself in handling stress?

What do you commit to regarding downtime and relaxation?

Which voices do you want to remember NOT to listen to?

What do you want to direct your attention toward and away from?
Which of conditioning's scams do you want to keep a close eye on in order to avoid?

You need to cancel your appointment for a massage. It's expensive and self-indulgent.

If you sign up for those classes you'll be the oldest and least prepared person in the room.

Why don't you have a couple of beers and watch the game on TV? You can do yoga in the morning.

Where was your attention when the bell rang to end meditation? You were off in fantasyland again, weren't you?

These people don't like you. You don't fit in here. You should have stayed at home.

Why would anyone want to date you? You're needy, boring and unattractive.

Which hole in the sidewalk does egocentric karmic conditioning talk you into stepping into over and over?

What reminders will help you sidestep that hole?

What attitude of mind do you choose for yourself? Peace? Calm? Relaxation?

Do you want to remember to "stop, drop, and breathe"?

How will you remember to celebrate your successes?

What special compliments and praise make your heart sing?

How will you take care of yourself in difficult relationships?

What words of encouragement do you need to hear almost constantly?

--Reminders for caring for the heart and spirit:

What makes your heart feel good?

How will you make sure your life includes lots of what makes your heart feel good?

What inspires you? Poetry? Music? Guidance from wise teachers?
Nature?

--Reminders for staying present:

What can distract you?

How do you forget yourself?

What does your awareness practice need to consist of?

How will you support yourself in keeping your commitments to waking up and ending suffering? Do you respond best to reading, listening, guided imagery, solitude, quiet time in nature?

These are simply some jumping off points to launch your own creativity. The aim here is this:

If you could be surrounded every day
by all the wisdom, love, and compassion
in the universe,
what would that look and sound like?

If the Buddha
(or your favorite compassionate being)
were walking around with you all the time,
supporting, nurturing,
encouraging, guiding, mentoring,
what would you be seeing and hearing?

With a little attention and awareness you will realize you know the answer to that question. You know what kind of support you need to have the life you know is available to you. The fact that you know that means you can provide it. And, the fast track to providing it for yourself is through a personal coaching program in which you guide and direct yourself to do, have, and be everything you need to live a life beyond suffering.

Your recording will be a powerful implement for replacing practicing what
you *don't* want
with practicing what
you *do* want.

YOUR RECORDING: THE PROCESS

It would seem a simple thing in this age of micro-devices to make a recording and carry it around with you, wouldn't it? But the voices of self-hate can talk us out of it, wipe from consciousness any memory of our desire to do it, and, if sometime later we do remember, beat us mercilessly for forgetting. So it's crucial to take making the recording out of the hands of self-hate.

Any portable recording device will do if it has ample space for what you want to put on it, is easy for you to use, and accommodates earbuds. I got my recorder from Radio Shack. It's a relatively inexpensive digital recorder that fits in my pocket and has no bells and whistles. The only extras are earbuds and one AAA battery. I could use an app for my iPhone for this project, or I could put the whole thing into iTunes or similar software.

Until you get started, you might hear voices saying...

Please trust me on this: If you do it, you will love it, it will not be hard work, and you will have an experience of your heart responding in a way that will likely surprise you A LOT.

Every aspect of this practice is a personal choice. It's for you; make it be the way you want it to be. My encouragement in the process department is the same encouragement I give everywhere, all the time:

DON'T BELIEVE THE VOICES!

At this juncture they will hammer you with any limitations you are willing to believe:

"You're not tech savvy. You don't know how to do that stuff and it's too late for you to learn. You're just going to waste a bunch of time and money on one more thing that isn't going to work."

None of that is true, and if you consider it for a moment you'll see that what the voices are saying is just a variation on the old themes they use to stop you in other areas of life.

My first recording was done in fits and starts. I would think of something I wanted to say, record it, turn the recorder off, and wait for the next inspiration. This resulted in a recording full of end-of-track beeps and I constantly had to hit the "play" button. Plus, the tracks were at varying volumes—it just wasn't right! Eventually I typed out everything from each of the tracks and recorded them in cohesive units. If I want to listen to quotes I find inspiring, I go to that track. If I want to hear those reminders about how I want to be in life, I choose that track. Truth is, I listen to them all at least once a day, usually more often. I listen to some of them as I do yoga, to others while driving and, most days, to the whole thing in the morning as I get ready for the day.

I think you'll notice that your subpersonalities will love the recording. What they need, the only thing that will ever satisfy them, is your attention. No one else's attention—yours. They love to hear your voice talking to them with

lovingkindness and compassion about themselves
and their life. They have such a sad history of
being beaten up by the voices of egocentric
karmic conditioning/self hate; they long for and
will be healed and
freed by this simple
act of unconditional
love and acceptance:
making and listening to
a recording.

WHO MAKES THE RECORDING?

I hope when people record their practice reminders that those reminders and reassurances come from center, not from ego. We want to go to conscious awareness in making choices about what to record because those practices remind us who we really are and what we want to focus on, what we want our life to stand for, what we want to give our energy to, and who we want to be in life. Then when we do those practices—when we listen to that recording—it takes us back to that place.

For example, when you turn on the recorder and listen to "I want to meditate every day because meditation helps me remember who I am," it creates a gap in the constant stream of conversation from egocentric karmic conditioning. You remember that meditating helps you focus. You're calmer, kinder to people. You remember that even though the voices want to talk you out of it, it's really important to meditate every day. Listening to yourself saying you want to meditate because meditation helps you remember who you are, brings you back to that centered place, even though it's two weeks, a month, a year after you were moved to add that to your recording.

The more we listen to our recordings, the more we recognize that centered place as who we are and the more bogus egocentric karmic conditioning conversation sounds. From that centered place we can begin to hear:

"Oh, those voices, they just repeat and repeat and repeat. It's not helpful and, actually, I'm not listening to it—which means I'm not caught up in it! Which means I must be something different from what I always thought I was! I'm beginning to sense the difference between my authentic being, that which animates me, and that conditioned tape loop, that bizarre tapestry of misinformation the voices tell me I am."

Making a recording is not presented as a replacement for meditation practice, but it can be a step along the way to freedom from the bondage and suffering of egocentric karmic conditioning/self-hate. Freeing oneself from the grip of egocentric karmic conditioning/self-hate is the beginning of the joyous process of spiritual practice. Remember, awareness practice/spiritual practice does not begin until the beatings stop.

MAKING THE RECORDING:
MONASTERY DISCUSSION

Cheri: Someone please remind the group what our homework was.

1st person: We were asked to make a recording of things that we want to remember that we sometimes forget. These are reminders from our own internal mentor, in our voice, about what's important to us.

Cheri: Yes, what an awareness practice coach would say, walking around next to you reminding you what's important, what you value, what you want to give your attention to, what you want to remember...even what you want to avoid, if you choose that direction. It becomes a replacement for the constant yammering of self-hate many folks live with.

2nd person: At your suggestion, two months ago I made one of these recordings and have been listening to it almost every day and it's having a profound effect on me. Some of the things on the recording are awarenesses I've had. For instance, I heard a voice say "I wish this were different," referring to my life, and in that moment I disidentified from it. I could see that there was nothing wrong with anything in that moment. And so the very last thing on my recording is "I wish this were different is a lie. I wish this were different is conditioning. Everything is okay right now." Listening to my recording is like having you with me because these are the kinds of things you have said so often. I love it.

Cheri: That's a perfect example of how making the recording can benefit us. Conditioning says awful things to folks hundreds of times a day, and it's good to be able to say, whoa, that's not a good message to be listening to! And yet, without awareness, those messages go through and we believe them. We don't realize the profound effect they have on us. It's powerful brainwashing. And so to acknowledge "That's a lie. I hear that voice often. It says blah blah blah, but it's not true! I commit to not believing that. I'm not going to live from that place. What I know to be true is...." And then give myself that information over and over.

We all know that we can have an awareness and conditioning will begin immediately to close over it. Many people report that they see something profound and years later they have the same awareness and think, oh, I had forgotten. But it doesn't have to be that way. If we have an internal mentor in our ear, reminding us several times a day of what we know to be true for us, we tend not to lose track of the awarenesses we have. A powerful tool conditioning has is the ability to distract us from what we want to remember so that it can be in control, talking to someone who believes what it says. Having a steady reminder of what we want to remember is a very good thing.

THIRTY DAYS
OF EXERCISES
TO INSPIRE CREATION
OF YOUR RECORDING

A
SELF-GUIDED
WORKSHOP

There is little agreement as to the number of times we need to practice something before it becomes habitual, some say 15 days, some 21 days, others say 30. Thirty seems such a nice, round, month-ish sort of number that we're going to choose it. We will borrow some good suggestions from the 30-day retreat in our book *Making a Change for Good*, such as, you will need:

-- a journal or notebook.
It can be as simple or as fancy as you like; it is important that the one using it likes it.

-- a time and place to do this work.
The place can be anywhere you feel comfortable. The time needs to be once in the morning, once in the evening.

-- a sense of humor, the willingness to be compassionate, and some patience.

Choose an exercise at the beginning of the day. Focus on the exercise throughout the day. At the end of the day, jot down in your journal what you've seen, looking for anything you might want to add to your recording.

Add your insights to your recording.

Do these exercises in any order. Stay with one exercise for several days if you choose. Alter them in any way that feels right to you in the moment. If you are inspired to make up your own exercises, please do so.

There is often room on these pages to write a response to the exercise. Consider using this book as a journal if you would like.

Now, choose one of the exercises from pages 136 through 165 and begin the journey.

"How I Want My Life to Be"

Find a quiet time and place and repeat the "How I want my life to be" imagery from page 80.

Add to your recording:
What are you feeling when you are having the life you want to have?
Where do you feel that in your body?
What words express the feeling?

Statements of Intention

Read pages 41-43 of this book into your recorder. Add anything else that speaks to your heart as helpful.

Many Questions

Review pages 115-118, part of the "Making Your Recording" section. Notice which of the many questions speak to you today (tomorrow might be different).

Consider the questions as you go about your day, journal your responses, and add them to your recording.

Awareness Word or Phrase of the Day

Choose a word or phrase for the day that will
remind you to practice turning your attention to
how you want your life to be. Write it down and
take it with you everywhere you go. Each time
you see it, turn your attention to where you
want it to be. If you have trouble remembering
to look at your word or phrase, set an alarm or
write it on your hand or...

Examples:
Kindness
I choose peace and calm.

Add the word or phrase to your recording and
remind yourself of its purpose for the day.

You can repeat this one daily.

A Reminder to Direct the Attention

As mentioned earlier, perhaps the most difficult aspect of awareness practice in the beginning is remembering to do it. Decide what you're going to do to remind yourself that what you want is to direct your attention to how you want your life to be.

Examples:
Every time I open a door
Every time I see the color red
Every time I hear music

Add your reminders to the recording.

These reminders can be changed daily.

"I Wish Someone Had Told Me..."

Most of us didn't get a lot of mentoring growing up about how to be or what to do. The process of socialization tends to be one of reprimands for doing something "wrong" rather than instructions for doing things "right." When you look at your life, what are some pieces of information you wish someone had told you before you had to find out the hard way?

Here are some suggestions. Add your own.
-- It's good to be the person you want to find.
-- Hard work doesn't guarantee you'll get what you want.
-- Even good relationships take maintenance.
-- You can occasionally dislike someone you love.
-- It's okay to have emotions.
-- Honesty, with yourself in particular, is the best policy.

Add the list and any insights from your responses to the recording.

139

What Is Your Color?

Allow to arise in conscious awareness, a response to this question:

What is the color you're most drawn to?

(See if you can not entertain voices that want to argue about what arose.)

As you go through your day, each time you see that color let it bring you back to your experience of how you want your life to be.

Add your responses to this exercise to your recording.

The Sensations of the Life You Choose

Turn your attention right now to the place in your body that you feel the sensations of the life you choose.

Picture those sensations in "your color"...

Add your responses to this exercise to the recording.

The Color of Center

Recall a time when you felt centered...

What color "goes with" that experience?

As you go about in daily life and see the color,
practice using it as a reminder to come back to
center, to how you want your life to be.

Add what you see in this exercise to your
recording.

Getting Dressed as Awareness Practice

Today when you get dressed*, be aware of which part of you is picking out what to wear. What are the emotions, projections, and conversation behind the choice?

When the choice has been made, decide to wear something else. What happens?

Add what you see about your process to your recording.

*It's fun to note the order of dressing, and then to change it up.

Other People's Clothes

Watch today what you project onto people based on what they're wearing. Who do you think they are? Follow that projection back to that part of yourself. (Yes, that is you, too.)

Add what you see about your process to your recording.

Been Bamboozled Lately?

Which voices have been able to bamboozle you lately? What scams have you fallen for? Do you have a sense of how you get talked into believing them? Are there circumstances you're aware are conducive to a "voices take-over"? For instance, is it easier for them to get to you when you're tired? Hungry? Stressed?

Examples of some common bamboozles:
"I'm tired. Time for coffee and doughnuts. I'll feel much better."
"It's time to meditate, but I'll just quickly check my email first."
"I know it's probably not good for me, but I want... [fill in what the voices say to you]."

Add what you see in this exercise to your recording.

"How Do You Know That?"

Watch the beliefs and assumptions about who and how you are that show up. They're difficult to see because they show up as "truth." Each time you hear a voice in your head giving you information about you (or someone else, or the world, or...), ask the voice, "How do you know that?" Followed by, "Who says so?"

It can be helpful to do this exercise with a journal that you carry during the day. Jot down the suspected false beliefs and assumptions, unexamined opinions, and iffy perspectives you watch come into your head and/or out of your mouth.

Add what you see about your process to your recording.

Other People's Projections

As you go about your day, listen to other people's projections. (Don't tell them what you're doing, and certainly don't use their projections against them!)

Notice what you project onto the people whose projections you're listening to. Pay particular attention to whether or not you project that they feel about you the way you feel about yourself. Then, notice which "self" you're identified as.

Add what you see about your process to your recording.

Relationship with the Mentor

Find a quiet place to sit for a while. Close your eyes and attend to your breath. When you feel ready, allow an image of your mentor to come into conscious awareness. Notice how it feels to be with the mentor.

Continuing to relax and breathe, explore all the ways and places you feel the mentor's presence in your body, emotions, and mind. Sitting quietly together like old, very dear friends.

Add to your recording:
"When I'm with the mentor I feel...." and any other reminders you'd like about your relationship with the mentor.

Drawing the Mentor

Draw a picture of your mentor.

If the voices have you convinced you can't draw, find a good likeness in a magazine. Better yet, draw the picture with your non-dominant hand*.

Note the self-talk and ask your mentor for encouragement and support.

Add the process you did around this exercise to your recording.

*If you're right-handed, use your left hand to draw and write. If you're left-handed, use your right hand to draw and write. Doing this often helps us to get outside our usual ways of thinking.

Talking with the Mentor

Write a non-dominant hand dialogue with your mentor.

For example:
Non-dominant hand writes: Dear Mentor...
Dominant hand (mentor) writes: Dear (your name)...

When doing this exercise it's vital to keep a sharp eye on egocentric karmic conditioning. It will slip in before you know it!

Add your insights from this dialogue to your recording.

Interacting with the Mentor

Allow a couple of subpersonalities who were present recently to have a dialogue with the mentor.

A short example:
Marshmellow: I was scared when I got yelled at.
Mentor: I'm sorry you felt scared. Can I help?
And so on...

Add this dialogue to your recording.

Conscious, Compassionate Mentoring

What issue in your life, if you could change your relationship with it through conscious, compassionate mentoring, would bring you the most freedom and peace?

Remember, these are *process* exercises. Start with something small, get the hang of mentoring/ being mentored, and slowly move toward that issue that would bring you the most freedom and peace. Such as:

1) I'm going to get enough sleep.
2) I'm going to meditate for at least a few minutes each day.
3) I will listen to my recording at least once a day.

Add your experiences with this exercise to your recording.

Messages from Childhood

Which messages from childhood do you trip over most often?

Examples:
-- If I'm kind to others they'll be kind to me.
-- Keeping my ideas to myself is best.
-- I am judged by what I accomplish.

Add to your recording reminders of what you need to remember to step free of this conditioning.

Examples:
-- When I am kind to me it helps me be kind to others.
-- I have compassion for myself no matter what.

Reassurances

Messages from childhood are still being received by a child, a young aspect of the personality. Each time you hear or recall one of those messages, offer a reassurance to the young subpersonality who was traumatized by and still suffers with the cruel judgment accompanying the message. Remember, a reassurance is usually a message from the mentor to a child.

Ask a young, suffering part of you what she or he would like to hear that would be reassuring. Reassurances are often simple and direct. Examples:
1) I'm here with you. You are not alone.
2) You're perfect just as you are.
3) I love you exactly as you are.

Add your experiences with this exercise to your recording.

Typical Conversations

Write down a typical conversation you hear in your mind about someone. Choose one that repeats often enough that you know the dialogue well. Example: "He's the most confident and creative person I know. He doesn't let little things bother him. He has things in perspective. I wish I were like him." (Write out the conversation before reading on.)

Now, own that what you wrote about another person are your projections. They are who *you* are. Your projections might or might not be true for that person, but they are certainly true for the person whose head they appear in. In awareness practice this is a huge step. And remember also, NO JUDGMENTS! (Judgments of you are **projections** from egocentric karmic conditioning/self-hate.)

Add your experiences with this exercise to your recording.

Another Typical Conversation

Recall a conversation in your head that you typically get caught up in and suffer as a result.

Write it out and break it down into:
Beliefs
Assumptions
Projections
Egocentric karmic conditioning
Self-hate

Now, write out what you see to be true instead.

Add your experiences with this exercise to your recording.

Watch out for bamboozles here, too. "But it's TRUE...!"

Just for You

Write out your own guided meditations and imageries of any length, saying things that bring you back to the experience of life you want to have.

Read these into your recorder. It is also fun to record impromptu guided meditations and imageries.

When to Listen

For the next several days, listen to your
recording:
1) as you prepare for the day
2) while driving
3) while doing simple chores
4) when you're enjoying hobbies, such as
gardening or tinkering with something
5) when...?

Add to your recording any insights about
incorporating listening to it into more of your
daily activities.

Bits and Pieces

Notice whether or not you spontaneously remember bits and pieces of your recording as you go about the day.

Add to your recording what you've noticed has been most supportive of bringing these reminders into your daily life.

Stumbling Blocks

Here are examples of stumbling blocks to making and listening to your recording that might be thrown in your path by egocentric karmic conditioning/self-hate:

"too much to do"
"this isn't working"
"don't feel like it"

Notice any quiet little under-the-radar, one-liner stumbling blocks. As you become aware of them, write them down in your journal. Add them to your recording so that as you listen they lose the power to subvert your efforts.

(What other places do these stumbling blocks keep you from the life you want to have?)

Music

Is there music that helps bring you back to center? If so, record that.

Many lyrics feed the voices of self-hate, giving messages along the lines of "without you I'm nothing, now that you're gone my life stinks, and the ever popular, you don't want me I might as well kill myself." Spend a little time altering some of these songs to speak to your heart. Perhaps something like, "Now that I've found me..." and "I am the sunshine of my life."

Inspirational Quotes

Remember to look for inspiring quotes that help bring you back to center to add to your recording.

Perhaps most important, add appreciation and expressions of gratitude for yourself for being willing to do this challenging work of freeing a very good and deserving person from suffering.

"You can search throughout the entire universe for someone who is more deserving of your love and affection than you are yourself, and that person is not to be found anywhere. You, yourself, as much as anybody in the entire universe, deserve your love and affection."
-- The Buddha

Finished?

The voices will try to talk you into the notion that you're finished with an issue and don't need to listen to that part of the recording any more. Write down in your journal everything the voices say about:

-- how "past that" you now are
-- how hopeless you now are
-- how bored with the recording you are
-- how much "you" hate your voice
-- how "you" wish it were someone else's voice.

Don't fall for any of it! Just keep adding and listening.

PLEASE REMEMBER:

This is your recording,
your life,
and your awareness practice.

You cannot do it wrong. You cannot go astray
unless conditioned mind talks you into quitting.
And even that's not really a problem. You'll
remember sometime and that will be the
perfect time to start again.

If you do this series of exercises, at the end you
will have a powerful, game-changing, conditioning-
busting recording in your
own voice, saying things you
always wanted to hear, from
the only person whose
opinion really matters,
delivering reminders you
know will assist you toward
having the life you want.

A
GLOSSARY
WITH EXERCISES

WHAT IS AWARENESS PRACTICE?

The term "awareness practice" is perfectly
descriptive of what we are doing in the pursuit
of waking up and ending suffering. It
often seems odd to people, as do terms such as
meditation practice or spiritual practice.

Awareness practice is the process of dispelling
the illusion of separation, a "me" separate from
"the world." When we develop more subtle
awareness through meditation, guidance, and
spiritual work, we begin to see through the
illusion. The more we practice, the less
believable the illusion of separation becomes.

Egocentric karmic conditioning is not interested in
having conditioned people realize that what
they're attending to is not LIFE, but is in fact a
brain-washing loop of false information being
provided by egocentric karmic conditioning itself.
With awareness practice, we learn what being
present in life is and how to let go into that.

THE FOUNDATION OF AWARENESS PRACTICE

The primary tools of awareness practice are five processes:

1. SUBPERSONALITIES

2. BELIEFS AND ASSUMPTIONS

3. PROJECTION

4. DISIDENTIFICATION

5. CENTERING

That I have included definitions of these in almost all previous books is an indication of how important I find them to be.* These five processes are essential to seeing through the illusion of a self separate from life. I have also included descriptions of egocentric karmic conditioning, self-hate, and *True Nature* (ultimately not possible!).

*Even if you're familiar with these five processes, I encourage you to study this section.

1. SUBPERSONALITIES

This term refers to the various aspects of the self. As children, we formed new personalities in response to threatening circumstances. Being a compliant, quiet son isn't working? Become a protective fighter. Being an aggressive, angry daughter isn't working? Become a people-pleaser. Now, as adults, all of these aspects are potentially available as roles we can assume in different situations. Aspects of the self common to many include partner, sibling, parent, worrier, athlete, artist, cook, procrastinator, student, worker...the list is endless. The awareness that we are not one unchanging personality is a fundamental insight in Zen Buddhism.

EXERCISE

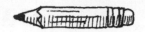

Consider for a moment ten or so of your most dominant ways of being in life. Choose some roles, but add some emotions as well. For instance, you may be an attorney or a clerk with a wide range of moods, but spend a lot of your life feeling grouchy. You could be an animal lover who has your primary experience of unconditional love with small, furry critters. Once you've made your list, look to see what quality each of these subpersonalities embodies.

2. BELIEFS AND ASSUMPTIONS

We all hold many, many unexamined beliefs and unconscious assumptions. Again, as children, we adopted these as ways to survive. In fact, each subpersonality is an expression of a belief. "If I become who my parents want me to be, they will love me the way I need them to" is an example of a belief. "No one is going to take care of me so I'm going to do whatever it takes to take care of myself" is another. When we operate from a belief without realizing it, we can get bogged down in suffering for a long time. Practicing every-moment awareness brings to light our beliefs and assumptions, enables us to let them go, and ends the suffering.

EXERCISE

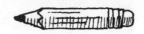

Without looking to conditioned mind to get the "right answers," fill in these blanks with as many responses as occur to you:

I believe _____.

I think _____.

Now, finish these sentences:

People are
The world is
Life can be
If only I could
Everyone should
I would never
I will enjoy my life when

Remember, these are beliefs, not truths.

3. PROJECTION

Understanding projection is the single most important tool of awareness practice. Simply stated, projection is the process of looking at the world and seeing ourselves. When we are unaware that all we ever see is ourselves, we suffer mightily. We believe that what we see "out there" is true out there but not within us. For example, we project greed and dishonesty onto a politician and fail to own those traits in ourselves. Everyone projects. There's nothing wrong with projection—it's just what we do. But if we don't know that "what I see is who I am," we can be caught in that bizarre tapestry of misinformation from which it can be extremely difficult to escape. The practice of owning our projections acts as a clear mirror in which to see ourselves.

What I see is who I am.

EXERCISE

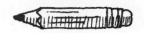

Answer the following:

What is the most beautiful sight you've ever seen?
What is the most glorious sound you've ever heard?
What is the most delicious taste?
What is the most wonderful feeling?
What does love feel like?

You projected those; they came from inside you. To have an experience of that, write down as you allow yourself to take in:
I (say your name if you like) am beauty.
I am the source of, I project, the beauty I see.
I am the experience of glorious sound.
I am the creator of delicious taste.
I am all the wonderful feelings I feel.
I am love.

4. DISIDENTIFICATION

This is the process of "waking up" (becoming aware of) and "stepping back from" (letting go of) subpersonalities, beliefs and assumptions, and projections. For example, your boss is talking to you about an intractable problem at work. You have what you think is a simple solution, but you're afraid to speak up because you're identified with a young subpersonality who believes that if she makes waves she will get into trouble. With practice, you can learn to "step back," recognize the subpersonality and the belief, and step into center, leaving you free to say or not say something to your boss. Without the skill of disidentification, we can spend a long time believing that the perceptions (projections) of the subpersonality we are identified with are "true" and "real," and we suffer as a result.

In awareness practice it is crucial to discern when we are identified with a subpersonality. A world of confusion and suffering is dispelled when we say, "Oh, I see. I'm identified with _____. That's really all that's going on. I can step back into center."

EXERCISE

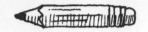

Consider which 3 aspects of yourself you would most like to disidentify from, leaving you free to care for them rather than acting out of them.

1)

2)

3)

Make a list of what you know about each of these parts of yourself. For instance, what do you talk to yourself or others about when identified with each of these personalities? How old do you feel emotionally? How does the world look to these individuals? The fellow in the little cartoon is identified with an impatient, angry part of himself who hates being stopped by traffic. (I project!)

Your lists might look something like this:

I keep repeating that I really hate this.
I don't want this to be happening.
If only I hadn't said that I wouldn't be having
this experience.
People hate it when I say things like that.
I feel awful.
No one is going to like me now.
I feel like I felt in middle school.
The world looks big and scary.
Everyone is more powerful than I am and they
don't like me!

When we begin to recognize aspects of the
personality with which we regularly identify, we
increase our odds of realizing what's causing our
suffering. In that moment of realization, we
can step free of the identification. The fellow in
the cartoon had **disidentified** when he said, "Oh,
wait. I know this guy."

5. CENTERING

Center is that "place" where there is only experience but no separate self to be having the experience. It is where there is no identification with an "I" who feels separate from what is and is suffering. It is the core of wisdom, love, and compassion that is the True Nature of all things. Other terms for center include "Brahman," "God within," "the Tao," "the Ground of Being." Center can be hidden from us by the insistent voices of conditioned mind, but, with willingness and practice, we can learn to step back at will in each moment, reuniting ourselves with intrinsic purity.

INTRINSIC PURITY

EXERCISE

What does "center" mean to you? When have
you felt it? How does it feel? Relaxed?
Peaceful? Comfortable? Expansive?

EGOCENTRIC KARMIC CONDITIONING

Egocentric karmic conditioning creates and maintains an imaginary world, a parallel universe, in which its reality is, second by second, compared to life as it actually is.

egocentric karmic conditioning
conditioned mind
conditioning
ego-self
ego

} SAME THING

Each of us arrives at our current incarnation propelled by certain karmic tendencies or predispositions. We talk about this as, "you are the sum total of everything it has taken to produce you since before the beginning of beginningless time." The entire universe comes together in you; the influences brought to bear are vast and ancient.

Quickly the new-born little package of tendencies

grows enough to encounter the beliefs, assumptions, projections, and expectations of a particular societal structure, usually parents and family. When those worlds collide, the karmic predispositions must be altered to accommodate the demands of the present circumstances if this nascent individual is to survive. That survival is dependent on bringing all of life down to a personal relationship with the I/me/my of the fledgling ego-self. "What does this circumstance mean for my survival?" "What do I need to be/do right now in order to survive?" The voices learn to supply the answers to those questions, and they continue to supply answers far past the time those questions no longer needed to be asked. In fact, the less the voices are needed to supply information, the more strident they become.

The voices have gone from helping a child
making his way in an unknown world
to helping themselves to the life force
of a grown person.

And, they become increasingly hateful as we practice turning attention away from them. It is now "their" survival that is dependent upon the attention they receive from the rightful owner of the life force that fuels their illusory existence.

The voices in your head insisting that something is wrong and that you need to be different are egocentric karmic conditioning.

Within ourselves, we can observe how egocentric karmic conditioning operates like a gossip magazine, a radio talk show, or a 24-hour cable "news" station dependent for its survival on grabbing and keeping the attention of listeners. Because it requires an uninterrupted flow of increasingly shocking, disturbing, and inflammatory information to capture the attention, the purveyors are constantly on the look-out for the next horrifying happening, real or made up.

Here are two examples of the almost limitless manifestations of egocentric karmic conditioning. The first is about "urgency," the second, "control."

"Amanda "
Amanda is driven to get as much done as possible every day. She has a to-do list that she'll never complete because five items are added for every one she checks off. The voices in her head pressure her to do more, go faster. A sense of urgency fills her body with adrenalin. Still, she needs several cups of coffee and doses of sugar throughout the day to keep up the pace. She takes pride in being a multi-tasker and describes herself as competent, and efficient. She doesn't sleep well and feels anxious most of the time.

Amanda is drawn to meditation, reads books about spirituality, is concerned about her health (she eats too much fast/junk food, could lose a few pounds, and wishes she had more time for exercise), and often creates plans to take better care of herself. She gets regular beatings about the bad choices she makes.

Before leaving for a morning meeting at work, there are the endless tasks to attend to, and she is running behind schedule as she races out the door. If traffic is good, she will just make it; if traffic is bad, she will be late. Suddenly, up ahead she can see that the traffic is at a dead stop, nothing moving. Pictures of the missed meeting and her boss's displeasure flood through her mind. As she scrambles for her phone, frantically coming up with the excuses, she hears, "Well, you did it again. You're late. You always do one more thing, the one thing that results in stuff like this. What's the matter with you? Aren't you ever going to learn?" And a mountain of misery descends on Amanda.

Here's the deal:
None of that happened to the real Amanda.
And the great sadness is that the authentic
Amanda was taught to believe all of that drama
is who she is. But, of course, it isn't and it
never was.

Aldous Huxley said, "The...knowledge of what we
really are accounts for our grief at having to
seem to be what we are not." The authentic
Amanda knows deep down, through the conscious
compassionate awareness that animates her,
that the life she's living is not really who she is.
She longs for something different, something she
can't exactly define, but that she senses would
fulfill her, make her happy. But she's been
convinced that she IS that frantic, anxious
person who tries so hard, often makes bad
decisions, and can never get it right, and that
the whole mess is her fault. If only she would
be different, be better, it would work out. But
she isn't better, and can't seem to be better,
and she despairs.

In that moment of despair there is possibility. Amanda could, in the quiet exhaustion following the beatings and defeat, decide to take her life in a different direction.

Conditioning will try to sabotage her at every turn, but with practice Amanda can end the drama.

"The Wall of Resistance"

It is difficult to tell the difference between egocentric karmic conditioning and authentic nature. It is so difficult that most people practice for years before realizing that the brick wall of resistance karmic conditioning uses to stave off awareness is not coming from them. For this reason, people who want to wake up and end suffering will choose to be in an environment that challenges conditioning so that they can see and hear it squawk its resistance.

The Zen Monastery Peace Center is just such an environment...

Many who come here are shocked at the level of resistance and discomfort produced by the challenge. I hear often from first-time visitors that they feel resistant to all the "rules and ritual." (I find this a bit humorous since, to me, our practice has few rules and ritual. We're closer to a Quaker style than to what is found in most Zen or Buddhist centers.) It's true that we have guidelines that newcomers may think of as rules, such as taking off shoes before entering a room, and we have them for two very good reasons. One is that guidelines are needed in community life; the other is that externally imposed guidelines bug egocentric karmic conditioning no end. **EGO**

The environment at the Monastery, because it is so foreign to our habitual patterns, requires us to pay constant attention, which is a quick trip to hell for conditioned mind. Conditioning wants to be in control of our experience. It wants the familiar, the known. Autopilot is the ideal way to fly. So when it gets insecure, annoyed, frightened, tired, bored, anxious, restless, dissatisfied, judgmental, or critical and builds its wall of resistance, it is difficult to see those reactions as coming from a threatened survival system working to protect its illusory reality rather than from a real person.

But if we are willing, attentive, kind, and patient, we begin to disidentify from conditioning's childish tantrums. We realize that authentic nature is the awareness that holds it all.

SELF-HATE

Self-hate is the glue that holds in place the illusion of a self separate from life. By convincing a person that there is something wrong and that it is their fault, self-hate can stay at the center of the universe, pretending to fix what's wrong, while sucking the life force out of that human.

The characteristics of self-hate are:

mean, nasty, hateful, vicious, belittling, undermining, sabotaging, cruel, judging, comparing, criticizing, humiliating, embarrassing, torturing, fear-mongering, catastrophizing, and all else that keeps attention focused in a way that generates the maximum amount of suffering.

Here is a process for counteracting self-hate. Modify as appropriate and apply any time the hateful voices attack:

What to Practice When You Wake Up in the Night and Self-Hate Is Trying to Kill You

If it's true, **acknowledge** that a part of you would rather be asleep, and then **accept** that you're awake.

Above all, **direct** the attention. **Commit** to not allowing the voices to take you down endless pathways to suffering.

Acknowledge your commitment and resolve.

Take a moment to **express appreciation to yourself** for being there with compassion and kindness to care for you when you need to be cared for.

Rejoice that you have this quiet time to be with yourself.

Focus on the breath, feeling the breath move through the body. Use the movement of the breath to relax the body. As the breath fills the chest, feel tension drain from the shoulders and neck. As the breath moves down through the legs, feel the muscles of the legs let go, allowing them to sink into the bed. Feel that same letting go and sinking with the back and the arms. Each breath allows the body to be heavier and more relaxed. Imagine the breath as a color and fill the body with that color. When the attention wanders, gently bring it back to the breath and feel the body let go and sink into the bed.

Ask yourself and Life questions and be open to the responses.

Examples of questions:
-- How do I want to feel? Focus on the breath moving in the body as you allow as much time as needed for the response to arise in conscious awareness.
-- When in my life have I had that feeling? Again, continue to focus attention on the breath

in the body, not allowing conditioned mind to grab the attention and give you its answers.
-- Where is that feeling in my body? Direct attention to that feeling. When attention wanders, bring it back. Remain patient. Bringing attention back to that feeling is often a moment-by-moment practice.

TRUE NATURE

True Nature, Authentic Nature, That Which
Animates, That Which Is...

When we step back from being identified with
conditioned aspects of ourselves, when we stop
believing the voices of self-hate, what's left is
who we really are, our True Nature. When we
step free of the conditioned sense of self, there
is only the constantly changing experience of life,
which we sense through awareness, without any
"self" at the center. There is only That Which
Animates us. Authentic being is simply present
in whatever arises in
each moment, without
judgment, analysis,
blame, fear, or any
dissatisfaction at all.

There Is Nothing Wrong With You
An Extraordinary Eight-Day Retreat
based on the book
There Is Nothing Wrong With You: Going Beyond Self-Hate
by Cheri Huber

Inside each of us is a "persistent voice of discontent." It is constantly critical of life, the world, and almost everything we say and do. As children, in order to survive, we learned to listen to this voice and believe what it says.

This retreat, held at the beautiful Zen Monastery Peace Center near Murphys, California, in the western foothills of the Sierra Nevada, is eight days of looking directly at how we have been rejecting and punishing ourselves and discovering how to let that go. Through a variety of exercises and periods of group processing, participants gain a clearer perspective on how they live their lives and on how to find compassion for themselves and others.

This work is challenging, joyous, fulfilling, scary, courageous, demanding, freeing, loving, kind, and compassionate—compassionate toward yourself and everyone you will ever know.

For information on attending, contact:
Living Compassion/Zen Monastery Peace Center
P.O. Box 1756
Murphys, CA 95247
Ph.: 209-728-0860
Fax: 209-728-0861
Email: thezencenter@livingcompassion.org
Website: www.livingcompassion.org

LIVING COMPASSION

To find out about our work with orphans in Zambia
and about purchasing gift cards and other products
to support that work,
visit www.livingcompassion.org.

* * *

ZEN MONASTERY PEACE CENTER

For a schedule of workshops and retreats and a list of our
meditation groups across the country,
contact us in one of the following ways.

Website: www.livingcompassion.org
Email: thezencenter@livingcompassion.org
Telephone: 209-728-0860
Fax: 209-728-0861

Zen Monastery Peace Center
P.O. Box 1756
Murphys, CA 95247

* * *

CHERI HUBER

For a schedule of retreats
and online classes with Cheri Huber
and archives of her call-in radio show,
visit www.cherihuber.com.

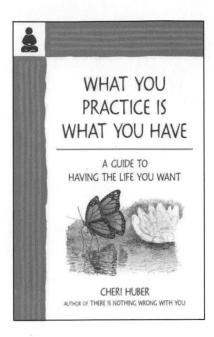

WHAT YOU
PRACTICE IS
WHAT YOU HAVE

A GUIDE TO
HAVING THE LIFE YOU WANT

CHERI HUBER
AUTHOR OF THERE IS NOTHING WRONG WITH YOU

What You Practice Is What You Have is a sequel to Cheri Huber's all-time bestseller, *There Is Nothing Wrong With You,* published in 1993. Over the years, many "There Is Nothing Wrong With You" retreats have been filled by those inspired by the book to look more deeply into how we can free ourselves from the ravages of conditioning and self-hate.

What You Practice Is What You Have further exposes the antics of conditioning and self-hate. Awareness practice tools, developed over the years by Cheri and the monks at the Zen Monastery Peace Center, are included.

REGARDLESS OF WHAT YOU WERE TAUGHT TO BELIEVE...

THERE IS
NOTHING WRONG
WITH YOU

GOING BEYOND SELF-HATE
A COMPASSIONATE PROCESS FOR LEARNING TO
ACCEPT YOURSELF EXACTLY AS YOU ARE

CHERI HUBER

Both titles will be available as e-books.

What You Practice Is What You Have
ISBN 0-9710309-7-9

There Is Nothing Wrong With You
ISBN 0-9710309-0-1

You can follow
"Cheri Huber's Practice Blog"
at
www.blogger.com.

Visit www.livingcompassion.org to:

--Sign up to receive notice of new email classes from Cheri Huber

--See a schedule of workshops and retreats at the

Zen Monastery Peace Center in Murphys, CA.

--Sign up for workshops and retreats

--Read blogs with updates from

the Africa Vulnerable Children Project in Zambia

--Sign up for Reflective Listening Buddies

--Sign up for Practice Everywhere

--Participate in the Sangha Market

--Buy CDs of Cheri Huber talks

AND MUCH MORE

TALK WITH CHERI

Online Classes

Cheri Huber conducts interactive online classes via e-mail
on a wide variety of subjects
related to Zen awareness practice.
To be notified of future classes
sign up at www.livingcompassion.org.

Open Air
Talk Radio

Open Air is Cheri Huber's weekly, internet-based,
call-in radio show.
Find out how to listen and participate at
www.livingcompassion.org.
Hear and download archived shows at www.cherihuber.com.

TRANSFORM
YOUR LIFE

A YEAR OF AWARENESS PRACTICE

CHERI HUBER
AUTHOR OF THERE IS NOTHING WRONG WITH YOU

ILLUSTRATED BY JUNE SHIVER

Here are 365 days of inspirational quotes and daily assignments
supporting spiritual practice. Few things in daily life help us to
be awake and aware. *Transform Your Life* is day-in-day-out
encouragement to find compassion for ourselves and all of life.

Published by Keep It Simple Books
All Cheri Huber titles are available through your local bookstore.
Distributed by Independent Publishers Group, Chicago
Transform Your Life is available as an iPhone app.